The Israel-Palestine Conflict

Middle East history, Volume 1

Michael Johnson

Published by Christopher Williams, 2024.

While every precaution has been taken in the preparation of this book, the publisher assumes no responsibility for errors or omissions, or for damages resulting from the use of the information contained herein.

THE ISRAEL-PALESTINE CONFLICT

First edition. March 23, 2024.

ISBN: 979-8224832286

Written by Michael Johnson.

Table of Contents

To those who strive for understanding and empathy in the face of conflict, this book is dedicated. May it serve as a beacon of knowledge and compassion, illuminating the path towards peace and reconciliation in the Israel-Palestine conflict.

Chapter 1: Introduction

The Israel-Palestine conflict stands as one of the most enduring and complex conflicts of the modern era, with roots deeply embedded in history, religion, nationalism, and geopolitics. This chapter serves as an entry point into the intricate web of narratives, grievances, and consequences that define this protracted struggle.

Brief Overview of the Israel-Palestine Conflict:

The conflict dates back to the late 19th and early 20th centuries, with the rise of competing national movements in the region. On one side, Jewish Zionists sought to establish a homeland in Palestine, driven by centuries of persecution and a desire for self-determination. On the other side, Palestinian Arabs, indigenous to the land, resisted what they saw as colonial encroachment and displacement.

The catalyst for the conflict can be traced to the Balfour Declaration of 1917, in which the British government expressed support for the establishment of a "national home for the Jewish people" in Palestine. This declaration laid the groundwork for Jewish immigration to Palestine and fueled tensions with the Arab population.

Following World War I, the British Mandate of Palestine was established, further intensifying Arab-Jewish tensions. Waves of Jewish immigration led to land acquisition and clashes with the Arab population, culminating in violence during the Arab Revolt of 1936-1939.

The United Nations Partition Plan of 1947 proposed the division of Palestine into separate Jewish and Arab states, with Jerusalem as an international enclave. While Jewish leaders accepted the plan, Arab leaders rejected it, leading to the Arab-Israeli War of 1948-1949, known to Palestinians as the Nakba, or "catastrophe." The war resulted in the establishment of the State of Israel and the displacement of hundreds of thousands of Palestinians, who became refugees in neighboring countries.

Subsequent Arab-Israeli wars, including the Six-Day War (1967) and the Yom Kippur War (1973), further reshaped the geopolitical landscape of the region, with Israel occupying the West Bank, Gaza Strip, East Jerusalem, and the Golan Heights. The status of these territories and the plight of Palestinian refugees remain central issues in the conflict.

Importance of Understanding Origins and Impacts:

Understanding the origins of the Israel-Palestine conflict is essential for grasping its enduring nature and the complexities involved in finding a resolution. Historical narratives, competing claims to land and identity, and the legacy of colonization all contribute to the layers of the conflict.

Moreover, the impacts of the conflict extend far beyond the borders of Israel and Palestine, affecting regional stability, global geopolitics, and human rights. The conflict serves as a rallying point for extremist groups, fuels anti-Semitic and anti-Arab sentiments, and perpetuates cycles of violence and mistrust.

At its core, the Israel-Palestine conflict represents a struggle for self-determination, security, and dignity for both Israelis and Palestinians. Addressing the root causes of the conflict and understanding its multifaceted impacts are crucial steps toward achieving a just and lasting peace in the region.

Outline of the Book's Structure:

This book aims to provide a comprehensive examination of the Israel-Palestine conflict, delving into its historical origins, geopolitical dynamics, human consequences, and prospects for resolution. The following chapters will explore various aspects of the conflict in greater detail:

1. Historical Background: Traces the roots of the conflict from ancient times to the modern era, examining the role of religion, nationalism, and colonialism.

2. Partition and Creation of Israel: Explores the events leading to the establishment of the State of Israel and the displacement of Palestinian refugees.

3. The Arab-Israeli Wars: Analyzes the major conflicts that have shaped the region, including the Suez Crisis, Six-Day War, and Yom Kippur War.

4. Palestinian Nationalism and Resistance: Examines the evolution of Palestinian national identity and the strategies of resistance against Israeli occupation.

5. Peace Processes and Diplomatic Efforts: Assesses the various attempts at peace negotiations, from the Oslo Accords to the failed Camp David Summit.

6. Settlements and Occupation: Investigates the growth of Israeli settlements in the occupied territories and the impact of occupation on Palestinian daily life.

7. Gaza Strip and Blockade: Examines the humanitarian crisis in Gaza, resulting from Israeli blockade and internal political divisions among Palestinians.

8. Jerusalem: Contested City: Explores the religious significance of Jerusalem and the challenges of sovereignty and access for Israelis and Palestinians.

9. External Influences and Regional Dynamics: Analyzes the role of neighboring Arab states, international actors, and regional conflicts in shaping the Israel-Palestine conflict.

10. Humanitarian Consequences: Investigates the social, economic, and psychological impacts of the conflict on civilians, including displacement, poverty, and trauma.

11. Media and Propaganda: Examines how media narratives and propaganda shape perceptions of the conflict and perpetuate stereotypes and biases.

12. Grassroots Initiatives and Civil Society: Highlights the role of grassroots movements, peacebuilding initiatives, and civil society organizations in fostering dialogue and reconciliation.

13. Future Prospects and Challenges: Assesses the challenges and opportunities for achieving a just and sustainable resolution to the conflict, including the prospects for a two-state solution or alternatives.

14. Conclusion: Reflects on the key themes and lessons learned from the exploration of the Israel-Palestine conflict and emphasizes the importance of continued dialogue, empathy, and international engagement in pursuit of peace.

Each chapter will provide in-depth analysis, historical context, and critical perspectives to offer readers a comprehensive understanding of the Israel-Palestine conflict and its broader implications. Through rigorous examination and thoughtful reflection, this book seeks to contribute to the ongoing conversation and efforts toward peace and justice in the region.

Chapter 2: Historical Background

The Israel-Palestine conflict is deeply rooted in centuries of history, with layers of religious, cultural, and political narratives shaping the present-day dynamics. This chapter delves into the ancient roots of the conflict, the period of Ottoman rule, and the emergence of Zionism under British mandate, culminating in the pivotal Balfour Declaration.

Ancient Roots of the Conflict: Biblical Narratives and Historical Claims

The land of Palestine holds immense significance in the religious traditions of Judaism, Christianity, and Islam. For Jews, the biblical narratives of the Hebrew Bible (Old Testament) establish a profound connection to the land of Israel, promised to Abraham and his descendants by God. The biblical accounts of the Exodus from Egypt, the conquest of Canaan, and the establishment of the Kingdom of Israel under King David and King Solomon are central to Jewish identity and collective memory.

Similarly, for Christians, the land of Israel holds significance as the birthplace of Jesus Christ and the setting for many key events in the New Testament. Jerusalem, in particular, is revered as the site of Jesus' crucifixion and resurrection, making it a focal point for Christian pilgrimage and devotion.

In Islam, the land of Palestine is revered as Al-Quds (Jerusalem), the third holiest site in Islam after Mecca and Medina. The Dome of the Rock and Al-Aqsa Mosque on the Temple Mount hold immense religious significance as the site from which the Prophet Muhammad is believed to have ascended to heaven during the Night Journey.

These religious narratives have not only shaped the spiritual connection of various communities to the land but have also fueled competing claims to sovereignty and territorial control. The intertwining of religious beliefs with political aspirations has contributed to the complexity and intractability of the Israel-Palestine conflict.

Ottoman Rule and the Rise of Zionism

For centuries, the land of Palestine was under the control of the Ottoman Empire, which ruled over a diverse array of ethnic and religious communities. Under Ottoman rule, Palestine was characterized by relative stability and religious pluralism, with Muslims, Christians, and Jews living side by side in urban centers like Jerusalem, Jaffa, and Hebron.

However, by the late 19th century, the Ottoman Empire was in decline, facing internal strife and external pressures from European powers. It was during this period of upheaval that the seeds of modern Zionism began to take root.

Zionism emerged as a political movement among European Jews seeking to establish a national homeland in Palestine. The term "Zionism" derives from Zion, a biblical synonym for Jerusalem, symbolizing the longing of the Jewish people to return to their ancestral homeland.

The father of modern political Zionism, Theodor Herzl, articulated the Zionist vision in his seminal work, "Der Judenstaat" (The Jewish State), published in 1896. Herzl argued for the establishment of a Jewish state as a solution to the problem of anti-Semitism in Europe, envisioning Palestine as the natural homeland for the Jewish people.

The First Zionist Congress convened in Basel, Switzerland, in 1897, marking the formal beginning of the Zionist movement. Delegates from various Jewish communities across Europe and the United States convened to discuss the practical implementation of Herzl's vision, including land acquisition, immigration, and diplomatic advocacy.

The rise of Zionism coincided with the emergence of nationalist movements across Europe and the Middle East, as ethnic and religious communities sought self-determination and independence. However, the Zionist project in Palestine was met with resistance from the indigenous Arab population, who feared displacement and loss of their own national identity and rights.

British Mandate and the Balfour Declaration

The collapse of the Ottoman Empire at the end of World War I ushered in a new era of colonialism and geopolitical reconfiguration in the Middle East. Under the terms of the Sykes-Picot Agreement (1916) and the Treaty of Sèvres (1920), the victorious Allied powers, namely Britain and France, carved up the former Ottoman territories into spheres of influence and mandates.

Palestine came under British control with the issuance of the British Mandate for Palestine by the League of Nations in 1922. The mandate entrusted Britain with the responsibility of administering Palestine and facilitating the establishment of a national home for the Jewish people, as outlined in the Balfour Declaration of 1917.

The Balfour Declaration, named after British Foreign Secretary Arthur Balfour, expressed support for "the establishment in Palestine of a national home for the Jewish people" while simultaneously affirming that "nothing shall be done which may prejudice the civil and religious rights of existing non-Jewish communities in Palestine."

The Balfour Declaration reflected the geopolitical calculations of the British government, which sought to garner support from the influential Zionist movement and Jewish diaspora, particularly in the United States. It also aimed to secure British interests in the Middle East, including access to strategic waterways and trade routes.

However, the Balfour Declaration ignited tensions between the Jewish and Arab communities in Palestine, as it promised the establishment of a Jewish national homeland on land inhabited by a predominantly Arab population. Arab leaders vehemently opposed the declaration, viewing it as a betrayal of their aspirations for self-determination and sovereignty.

The British Mandate period witnessed increasing tensions between Jewish and Arab communities, as competing nationalist movements clashed over land, resources, and political power. Arab revolts, Jewish immigration, and British attempts to maintain control exacerbated communal divisions and set the stage for future conflict.

In summary, the historical background of the Israel-Palestine conflict is characterized by the convergence of religious narratives, colonial interests, and nationalist movements. The ancient roots of the conflict, the rise of Zionism, and the impact of Ottoman rule laid the groundwork for the tumultuous events that would unfold under British mandate, culminating in the issuance of the Balfour Declaration. Understanding this historical context is essential for comprehending the complexities and enduring nature of the Israel-Palestine conflict.

Chapter 3: Partition and Creation of Israel

The partition of Palestine and the subsequent establishment of the State of Israel in 1948 represent a pivotal moment in the Israel-Palestine conflict, shaping its trajectory for decades to come. This chapter examines the United Nations Partition Plan of 1947, the Arab-Israeli War of 1948, and the profound consequences for both Israelis and Palestinians, including displacement, refugee crisis, and the birth of the State of Israel.

UN Partition Plan of 1947

In response to the escalating tensions between Jewish and Arab communities in Palestine, the United Nations proposed a partition plan to address competing claims to the territory. On November 29, 1947, the UN General Assembly adopted Resolution 181 (II), which called for the partition of Palestine into separate Jewish and Arab states, with Jerusalem designated as a corpus separatum under international administration.

The proposed Jewish state would comprise roughly 56% of Mandatory Palestine, while the Arab state would encompass the remaining 44%, with a population transfer suggested in certain areas to ensure demographic viability. The plan also included provisions for economic cooperation and the protection of minority rights in both states.

The UN Partition Plan was hailed by Zionist leaders as a historic opportunity to fulfill the long-held dream of a Jewish homeland, while Arab leaders vehemently rejected the proposal, viewing it as a violation of their rights and sovereignty. Arab states argued that the partition plan favored the Jewish minority and disregarded the rights of the Arab majority.

Despite objections from Arab states and Palestinian Arab leaders, the Jewish leadership in Palestine reluctantly accepted the partition plan, recognizing it as a stepping stone toward statehood. Jewish leaders saw the plan as a pragmatic compromise that provided international legitimacy for Jewish sovereignty in Palestine.

Arab-Israeli War of 1948

The adoption of the UN Partition Plan exacerbated tensions between Jewish and Arab communities in Palestine, leading to outbreaks of violence and conflict. In anticipation of the termination of the British Mandate on May 15, 1948, both Jewish and Arab militias began to mobilize, preparing for the impending struggle for control of the territory.

On May 14, 1948, David Ben-Gurion, the head of the Jewish Agency, declared the establishment of the State of Israel, proclaiming the fulfillment of the Zionist vision of a Jewish homeland. The declaration of independence was met with jubilation among Jewish communities worldwide, but it also sparked outrage and condemnation from Arab states and Palestinian Arabs.

The declaration of Israeli statehood was swiftly followed by the invasion of Palestine by neighboring Arab states, including Egypt, Jordan, Syria, and Iraq. The Arab League declared war on Israel, vowing to prevent the establishment of a Jewish state on Palestinian soil and to support the Palestinian Arab cause.

The Arab-Israeli War of 1948, also known as the War of Independence or Nakba (catastrophe) from the Palestinian perspective, lasted for over a year and resulted in significant casualties and displacement on both sides. The conflict witnessed intense fighting, including battles for control of key cities such as Jerusalem, Haifa, and Tel Aviv.

Despite being outnumbered and outgunned, the nascent Israeli Defense Forces (IDF) managed to repel the Arab armies and secure crucial victories on multiple fronts. Israeli forces also engaged in a campaign of ethnic cleansing, expelling hundreds of thousands of Palestinian Arabs from their homes and villages to ensure the establishment of a Jewish-majority state.

Establishment of the State of Israel and Palestinian Displacement

On May 14, 1948, following months of conflict and bloodshed, the State of Israel was formally established, with David Ben-Gurion serving as its first Prime Minister. The creation of Israel marked the realization of the Zionist dream of Jewish statehood after millennia of exile and persecution.

However, the establishment of Israel came at a staggering cost for the Palestinian Arab population. The Nakba resulted in the displacement of an estimated 700,000 Palestinians, who fled or were expelled from their homes and became refugees in neighboring Arab countries or internally displaced within Palestine.

The Palestinian refugee crisis remains one of the most enduring and unresolved consequences of the Arab-Israeli conflict, with millions of Palestinian refugees and their descendants still living in refugee camps across the Middle East, denied the right of return to their ancestral homes.

The Nakba continues to loom large in Palestinian collective memory, serving as a symbol of dispossession, displacement, and injustice. Palestinians commemorate Nakba Day annually on May 15, mourning the loss of their homeland and reaffirming their commitment to the right of return for Palestinian refugees.

In summary, the partition of Palestine and the establishment of the State of Israel in 1948 represent a defining moment in the Israel-Palestine conflict, with far-reaching consequences for both Israelis and Palestinians. The UN Partition Plan, the Arab-Israeli War of 1948, and the Nakba laid the groundwork for decades of conflict, displacement, and unresolved grievances, shaping the contours of the conflict to this day. Understanding this pivotal period is essential for comprehending the complexities and enduring legacies of the Israel-Palestine conflict.

Chapter 4: The Arab-Israeli Wars

The Arab-Israeli wars represent a series of conflicts that have profoundly shaped the political, military, and social landscape of the Middle East. From the Suez Crisis of 1956 to the Yom Kippur War of 1973, these wars have left an indelible mark on the region, exacerbating existing tensions and fueling cycles of violence and instability. This chapter explores the key events and consequences of the Suez Crisis, the Six-Day War, and the Yom Kippur War, and examines their lasting impact on the Middle East.

Suez Crisis (1956)

The Suez Crisis of 1956 was a pivotal moment in the history of the Middle East, marking a turning point in the dynamics of regional politics and the balance of power. The crisis was precipitated by a confluence of factors, including the nationalization of the Suez Canal by Egyptian President Gamal Abdel Nasser, Cold War rivalries, and imperial ambitions of Western powers.

In July 1956, Nasser announced the nationalization of the Suez Canal Company, which had been controlled by British and French interests since the late 19th century. The decision to nationalize the canal was motivated by Nasser's desire to assert Egyptian sovereignty and secure funding for the construction of the Aswan High Dam, a symbol of Egypt's modernization efforts.

The nationalization of the canal provoked outrage among British and French officials, who viewed it as a threat to their strategic interests and a challenge to their imperial authority in the region. In collusion with Israel, which harbored its own grievances against Egypt, British and French leaders hatched a plan to overthrow Nasser and regain control of the canal.

In October 1956, Israeli forces launched a preemptive invasion of the Sinai Peninsula, quickly seizing control of the territory and advancing toward the Suez Canal. British and French forces followed suit, launching coordinated military operations against Egyptian targets in the canal zone.

However, the invasion met with international condemnation and resistance from the United States and the Soviet Union, both of which viewed the intervention as a dangerous escalation of the Cold War. Under pressure from the international community, British, French, and Israeli forces were forced to withdraw from Egyptian territory, marking a humiliating defeat for the Western powers.

The Suez Crisis had far-reaching implications for the Middle East, underscoring the limitations of colonial intervention and the emergence of new power dynamics in the region. The crisis also solidified Nasser's stature as a charismatic leader and champion of Arab nationalism, cementing Egypt's role as a key player in regional politics.

Six-Day War (1967)

The Six-Day War of 1967 represents one of the most consequential conflicts in the history of the Arab-Israeli conflict, reshaping the geopolitical map of the Middle East and triggering decades of occupation, settlement, and resistance.

The origins of the Six-Day War can be traced to rising tensions between Israel and its Arab neighbors, particularly Egypt and Syria, in the years following the Suez Crisis. Disputes over territory, water resources, and Palestinian refugees fueled mutual hostility and mistrust, leading to sporadic clashes along the borders.

In May 1967, amid escalating tensions and military build-up, Egypt mobilized its forces in the Sinai Peninsula and expelled United Nations peacekeepers from the region, raising fears of an imminent confrontation with Israel. In response, Israel launched a preemptive strike against Egyptian airfields, decimating Egypt's air force and gaining air superiority within hours.

The rapid escalation of hostilities drew other Arab states, including Jordan and Syria, into the conflict, as they launched attacks on Israeli positions in the West Bank and the Golan Heights, respectively. Israeli forces responded with swift and decisive offensives, capturing vast territories from its Arab adversaries in a matter of days.

By the end of the Six-Day War, Israel had seized control of the Sinai Peninsula from Egypt, the West Bank from Jordan, and the Golan Heights from Syria, effectively tripling its territory and consolidating its dominance over the region. The war also resulted in the displacement of hundreds of thousands of Palestinian Arabs, who fled or were expelled from their homes in the newly occupied territories.

The Six-Day War had profound consequences for the Middle East, exacerbating existing tensions and laying the groundwork for future conflicts. The Israeli occupation of the West Bank and Gaza Strip, in particular, fueled Palestinian resistance and nationalist aspirations, setting the stage for decades of conflict and negotiation.

Yom Kippur War (1973)

The Yom Kippur War, also known as the October War or the Ramadan War, erupted on October 6, 1973, when Egypt and Syria launched coordinated attacks against Israeli positions in the Sinai Peninsula and the Golan Heights, respectively. The surprise assault caught Israel off guard and exposed vulnerabilities in its security apparatus, leading to intense fighting and significant casualties on all sides.

The Yom Kippur War was preceded by years of tension and failed diplomacy, as Arab states sought to regain territory lost in the Six-Day War and challenge Israeli hegemony in the region. Egypt's President Anwar Sadat and Syria's President Hafez al-Assad coordinated their efforts to launch a joint offensive against Israel, timed to coincide with the Jewish holiday of Yom Kippur, when Israeli defenses would be least prepared.

The initial Arab advances in the early days of the war dealt a psychological blow to Israel and its military establishment, as Egyptian and Syrian forces breached Israeli defenses and made significant territorial gains. However, Israel quickly mobilized its reserves and launched counteroffensives, pushing back Arab forces and regaining lost territory.

The Yom Kippur War witnessed intense and bloody battles on multiple fronts, including the Sinai Peninsula, the Golan Heights, and the Suez Canal. The conflict also saw the deployment of advanced military hardware, including Soviet-made weaponry supplied to Arab states and American-made equipment used by Israel, leading to significant casualties and destruction.

As the war entered its later stages, diplomatic efforts to broker a ceasefire and negotiate a resolution gained momentum, facilitated by international mediators such as the United States and the Soviet Union. A ceasefire agreement was eventually reached, and negotiations began to address the underlying grievances and territorial disputes between Israel and its Arab neighbors.

Impact of These Wars on the Region

The Arab-Israeli wars have had profound and enduring impacts on the Middle East, shaping the political, military, and social landscape of the region in significant ways.

Firstly, the wars have exacerbated existing tensions and fuelled cycles of violence and instability, perpetuating a state of perpetual conflict and insecurity for millions of people in the region. The ongoing occupation of Palestinian territories, the displacement of Palestinian refugees, and the expansion of Israeli settlements have all contributed to the perpetuation of the conflict and the entrenchment of mutual distrust and animosity.

Secondly, the wars have reshaped the geopolitical map of the Middle East, redrawing borders, altering alliances, and redefining power dynamics among regional actors. The defeat of Arab armies in successive conflicts has undermined the credibility of Arab nationalism and exposed the military vulnerabilities of Arab states, leading to a shift in the balance of power towards Israel and its Western allies.

Thirdly, the wars have contributed to the militarization of regional politics, as states invest heavily in military capabilities and alliances to defend against perceived threats and assert their interests. The proliferation of weapons and the escalation of arms races have further heightened tensions and increased the risk of conflict escalation in the region.

Fourthly, the wars have had profound social and human consequences, resulting in widespread displacement, trauma, and humanitarian crises. The displacement of Palestinian refugees, particularly as a result of the Six-Day War and the subsequent occupation of the West Bank and Gaza Strip, has created a protracted refugee crisis that continues to this day. Generations of Palestinians have grown up in overcrowded refugee camps, denied basic rights and opportunities, while their aspirations for statehood and self-determination remain unfulfilled.

Moreover, the wars have left deep scars on the collective psyche of populations across the region, fueling resentment, distrust, and intergenerational trauma. Families torn apart by conflict, communities devastated by violence, and individuals haunted by memories of loss and suffering bear witness to the enduring human cost of war.

Furthermore, the Arab-Israeli wars have had significant economic repercussions, diverting resources away from development and infrastructure and exacerbating poverty and inequality. The diversion of funds towards military expenditures, coupled with the disruption of trade and commerce, has hindered economic growth and development in the region, perpetuating cycles of dependence and underdevelopment.

The impact of the wars extends beyond the borders of Israel and its Arab neighbors, shaping regional geopolitics and global dynamics. The strategic importance of the Middle East, with its vast energy resources and strategic waterways, has made it a focal point of international competition and intervention, as major powers vie for influence and control.

The Arab-Israeli wars have also influenced broader trends in international relations, shaping alliances and coalitions, and influencing diplomatic strategies and policies. The United States, in particular, has emerged as a key player in the region, providing military, political, and economic support to Israel while seeking to maintain stability and secure its interests in the Middle East.

In summary, the Arab-Israeli wars have had far-reaching and enduring impacts on the Middle East, shaping its political, military, social, and economic landscape in profound ways. The legacy of conflict, displacement, and insecurity continues to cast a long shadow over the region, perpetuating cycles of violence and instability and hindering efforts towards peace, reconciliation, and development. Understanding the causes, consequences, and complexities of these wars is essential for comprehending the dynamics of the Arab-Israeli conflict and exploring pathways towards a just and sustainable resolution.

Chapter 5: Palestinian Nationalism and Resistance

The emergence of Palestinian nationalism and resistance movements has played a significant role in shaping the trajectory of the Israel-Palestine conflict. From the early stirrings of nationalist sentiment to the organized resistance against occupation, Palestinian aspirations for self-determination and sovereignty have been at the forefront of the struggle for Palestinian rights. This chapter explores the historical evolution of Palestinian nationalism, the pivotal role of the Intifadas, and the rise of militant groups such as Hamas.

Emergence of Palestinian Nationalist Movements

The roots of Palestinian nationalism can be traced back to the late 19th and early 20th centuries, as Palestinians began to assert their identity and demand recognition as a distinct national community. Under Ottoman rule, Palestinians inhabited a diverse society characterized by religious and cultural pluralism, but also faced increasing marginalization and discrimination.

The collapse of the Ottoman Empire and the subsequent British Mandate in Palestine provided fertile ground for the growth of nationalist movements, as Palestinians sought to resist foreign rule and assert their right to self-determination. Efforts to mobilize Palestinian political consciousness gained momentum in the interwar period, with the emergence of political parties, student organizations, and grassroots movements advocating for Palestinian rights.

The Arab Revolt of 1936-1939, sparked by Palestinian grievances against British colonial policies and Jewish immigration, marked a watershed moment in the development of Palestinian nationalism. The revolt, although ultimately suppressed by British forces, galvanized Palestinian resistance and laid the groundwork for future struggles against colonialism and occupation.

The Nakba of 1948, resulting in the displacement of hundreds of thousands of Palestinians and the establishment of the State of Israel, further fueled Palestinian nationalist sentiment and resistance. The loss of land, livelihoods, and homes became a rallying cry for Palestinians, igniting a sense of collective trauma and determination to reclaim their rights and homeland.

In the aftermath of the Nakba, Palestinian nationalism found expression through various political and social movements, including the Palestine Liberation Organization (PLO), founded in 1964 as the representative body of the Palestinian people. Led by figures such as Yasser Arafat, the PLO sought to unify Palestinian factions and coordinate resistance efforts against Israeli occupation.

Intifadas: First Intifada (1987-1993) and Second Intifada (2000-2005)

The First Intifada, or uprising, erupted in December 1987, sparked by widespread Palestinian frustration and anger over Israeli occupation, settlement expansion, and human rights abuses. Characterized by mass demonstrations, civil disobedience, and acts of resistance, the Intifada represented a grassroots mobilization of Palestinian resistance against Israeli rule.

Youth and women played pivotal roles in the First Intifada, organizing protests, boycotts, and strikes, and challenging the Israeli military presence in Palestinian towns and cities. The Intifada also witnessed the emergence of alternative political structures and institutions, such as popular committees and local councils, aimed at providing essential services and fostering community resilience.

The First Intifada garnered international attention and sympathy for the Palestinian cause, highlighting the injustices of Israeli occupation and the resilience of Palestinian resistance. The images of Palestinian youths throwing stones at Israeli tanks and soldiers became emblematic of the Intifada's spirit of defiance and determination.

The Oslo Accords, signed in 1993, marked the official end of the First Intifada and the beginning of a new phase in Israeli-Palestinian relations. However, the promises of Oslo, including the establishment of a Palestinian interim self-government authority, failed to materialize into meaningful progress towards Palestinian statehood and independence.

The Second Intifada, also known as the Al-Aqsa Intifada, erupted in September 2000, following a visit by Israeli politician Ariel Sharon to the Temple

Mount in Jerusalem, a site sacred to both Muslims and Jews. The visit, perceived as a provocation by Palestinians, triggered widespread protests and violence, escalating into a full-scale uprising against Israeli occupation.

The Second Intifada was characterized by a wave of suicide bombings, shootings, and attacks by Palestinian militants targeting Israeli civilians and military personnel. Israeli forces responded with harsh reprisals, including mass arrests, house demolitions, and targeted assassinations of Palestinian leaders.

The Second Intifada exacted a heavy toll on both Israelis and Palestinians, resulting in thousands of deaths and injuries on both sides. The cycle of violence and retaliation deepened mutual distrust and animosity, undermining prospects for peace and exacerbating divisions within Palestinian society.

Rise of Hamas and Other Militant Groups

The rise of Hamas, an Islamist militant organization, represents a significant development in the landscape of Palestinian resistance and nationalism. Founded in 1987 as an offshoot of the Muslim Brotherhood, Hamas emerged as a potent political and military force in the Gaza Strip, challenging the dominance of the secular nationalist factions represented by the PLO.

Hamas gained popularity among Palestinians disillusioned with the perceived corruption and ineffectiveness of the Palestinian Authority (PA) and the failure of the Oslo peace process to deliver tangible improvements in their lives. Hamas's network of social services, including schools, clinics, and charities, endeared it to many Palestinians, particularly in impoverished and marginalized communities.

Hamas's military wing, the Izz ad-Din al-Qassam Brigades, carried out numerous attacks against Israeli targets during the Second Intifada, including suicide bombings, rocket attacks, and kidnappings. The group's use of violence and its refusal to recognize Israel's right to exist have led to its designation as a terrorist organization by Israel, the United States, the European Union, and other countries.

In addition to Hamas, other militant groups such as Islamic Jihad and the Popular Front for the Liberation of Palestine (PFLP) have also engaged in armed resistance against Israeli occupation and settlement expansion. These groups, although smaller in scale compared to Hamas, have nonetheless played a significant role in shaping the contours of Palestinian resistance and nationalism.

The rise of militant groups like Hamas has further complicated efforts to achieve a negotiated settlement to the Israel-Palestine conflict, as their rejectionist stance and use of violence undermine prospects for dialogue and reconciliation. However, for many Palestinians, these groups represent a form of resistance against Israeli occupation and a means of asserting Palestinian rights and dignity in the face of oppression.

In summary, Palestinian nationalism and resistance have evolved over the decades in response to the challenges of occupation, displacement, and dispossession. From the early stirrings of nationalist sentiment to the organized resistance of the Intifadas and the rise of militant groups like Hamas, Palestinians have sought to assert their identity, reclaim their rights, and pursue their aspirations for freedom, justice, and self-determination. Understanding the complexities and dynamics of Palestinian nationalism and resistance is essential for comprehending the broader context of the Israel-Palestine conflict and exploring pathways towards a just and lasting peace in the region.

Chapter 6: Peace Processes and Diplomatic Efforts

The quest for peace between Israelis and Palestinians has been marked by numerous diplomatic efforts and peace processes, each aimed at resolving the long-standing conflict and achieving a just and lasting solution. From the historic Oslo Accords to the Camp David Summit and the Roadmap for Peace, this chapter examines the key diplomatic initiatives, their successes, challenges, and failures in advancing the cause of peace in the region.

Oslo Accords (1993)

The Oslo Accords, signed in 1993, represented a historic breakthrough in Israeli-Palestinian relations, marking the first direct negotiations between the two parties and laying the groundwork for a comprehensive peace agreement. Facilitated by secret negotiations in Oslo, Norway, between Israeli and Palestinian officials, the accords sought to address core issues such as the status of Jerusalem, Palestinian statehood, and the rights of refugees.

The Oslo Accords consisted of two main agreements: the Declaration of Principles (DOP), signed on September 13, 1993, and the Interim Agreement on the West Bank and Gaza Strip, signed in September 1995. The DOP outlined a framework for Palestinian self-government in the West Bank and Gaza Strip, with the establishment of the Palestinian Authority (PA) and the gradual transfer of powers from Israeli to Palestinian control.

The Interim Agreement, also known as Oslo II, delineated the division of responsibilities between Israel and the PA, including security, administration, and civil affairs. It also established a timetable for the withdrawal of Israeli forces from major population centers in the West Bank and Gaza Strip and the holding of Palestinian elections for the legislative council and president.

The Oslo Accords generated cautious optimism and hope for a peaceful resolution to the Israel-Palestine conflict, earning widespread international acclaim and recognition. However, the accords also faced criticism and skepticism from both Israeli and Palestinian hardliners, who viewed them as a betrayal of their respective national aspirations.

Despite the initial optimism surrounding the Oslo Accords, the peace process ultimately faltered due to a combination of internal and external factors, including political deadlock, violence, and mistrust. The assassination of Israeli Prime Minister Yitzhak Rabin by a Jewish extremist in 1995 and the breakdown of negotiations over final-status issues, such as Jerusalem and the right of return for Palestinian refugees, contributed to the unraveling of the peace process.

Camp David Summit (2000) and Taba Summit (2001)

The Camp David Summit of July 2000, convened by US President Bill Clinton and attended by Israeli Prime Minister Ehud Barak and Palestinian Authority President Yasser Arafat, represented a significant attempt to resolve the final-status issues of the Israel-Palestine conflict. The summit focused on contentious issues such as the borders of a future Palestinian state, the status of Jerusalem, and the fate of Palestinian refugees.

Despite intense negotiations and shuttle diplomacy by President Clinton, the Camp David Summit ended in failure, as the parties were unable to bridge the gaps on core issues. The status of Jerusalem, in particular, emerged as a major sticking point, with both sides laying claim to the holy city and refusing to compromise on their respective positions.

Following the collapse of the Camp David Summit, negotiations between Israeli and Palestinian officials continued at the Taba Summit in January 2001, facilitated by international mediators and diplomats. The Taba Summit witnessed further progress on key issues, with both sides making concessions and exploring creative solutions to longstanding disputes.

However, the Taba Summit ultimately ended without a final agreement, as the outbreak of violence and unrest, including the Second Intifada, undermined prospects for a negotiated settlement. The failure of the Camp David and Taba summits dealt a severe blow to the peace process and deepened mutual distrust and animosity between Israelis and Palestinians.

Roadmap for Peace (2003)

The Roadmap for Peace, initiated by the United States, the European Union, the United Nations, and Russia, represented a renewed effort to revive the stalled peace process and advance towards a two-state solution. Unveiled in 2003, the roadmap outlined a phased approach to resolving the Israel-Palestine conflict, with the ultimate goal of establishing an independent Palestinian state alongside Israel.

The roadmap consisted of three main phases: the cessation of violence and terrorism, the reform of Palestinian institutions, and the resumption of negotiations leading to a final-status agreement. It also called for confidence-building measures, including a freeze on Israeli settlement activity and the dismantlement of Palestinian militant groups.

Despite initial enthusiasm for the roadmap, implementation faced numerous obstacles and challenges, including ongoing violence, political instability, and lack of commitment from both sides. Israeli reluctance to halt settlement expansion and Palestinian infighting and corruption further hindered progress towards peace.

Challenges and Failures of Peace Negotiations

The peace negotiations between Israelis and Palestinians have been beset by numerous challenges and failures, reflecting the deep-seated mistrust, competing narratives, and entrenched interests on both sides. Among the key challenges are:

1. Security Concerns: Israeli concerns about security and the threat of terrorism have often overshadowed efforts to advance the peace process. The wave of suicide bombings and attacks during the Second Intifada reinforced Israeli fears and hardened attitudes towards concessions and compromises.

2. Settlement Expansion: The expansion of Israeli settlements in the occupied West Bank and East Jerusalem has been a major obstacle to peace negotiations, undermining the viability of a future Palestinian state and eroding trust between the parties. Despite international condemnation, Israeli governments have continued to authorize new settlement construction, further entrenching the occupation.

3. Political Divisions: Internal divisions within Israeli and Palestinian society have also hindered progress towards peace, as competing political factions pursue divergent agendas and priorities. In Israel, the coalition politics and ideological differences between left-wing and right-wing parties have complicated efforts to reach consensus on key issues. In the Palestinian territories, the split between

Fatah and Hamas has further fragmented Palestinian leadership and undermined efforts at unity and reconciliation.

4. Lack of Trust: Mutual mistrust and skepticism have been pervasive throughout the peace process, with both Israelis and Palestinians harboring deep-seated suspicions about each other's intentions and commitments. Decades of conflict, violence, and broken promises have eroded trust and confidence in the feasibility of a negotiated settlement.

5. Regional Instability: The broader regional context, including the rise of militant groups, proxy conflicts, and geopolitical rivalries, has also impacted peace negotiations between Israelis and Palestinians. Regional actors such as Iran, Hezbollah, and Hamas have sought to exploit the Israel-Palestine conflict for their own strategic interests, further complicating efforts to achieve peace.

In summary, the pursuit of peace between Israelis and Palestinians has been fraught with challenges, setbacks, and disappointments, reflecting the complexity and intractability of the conflict. Despite the efforts of international mediators, diplomats, and peace activists, the deep-rooted divisions and unresolved grievances between the parties continue to impede progress towards a just and lasting solution. However, the legacy of past peace efforts and the enduring commitment of stakeholders to the principle of peace offer glimmers of hope for a brighter future in the region.

Chapter 7: Settlements and Occupation

The growth of Israeli settlements in the West Bank and East Jerusalem stands as one of the most contentious and enduring aspects of the Israel-Palestine conflict. Rooted in a complex web of historical, legal, and geopolitical factors, the expansion of settlements has profound implications for the occupied Palestinian territories and the prospects for peace in the region. This chapter explores the growth of Israeli settlements, their legal and humanitarian implications under international law, and the responses of the international community to the ongoing occupation.

Growth of Israeli Settlements in the West Bank and East Jerusalem

Israeli settlements in the West Bank and East Jerusalem have been a central feature of Israeli policy since the capture of these territories during the Six-Day War of 1967. Initially portrayed as strategic outposts for security and defense, settlements have expanded rapidly over the decades, fueled by government incentives, ideological motivations, and religious fervor.

The settlement enterprise has been driven by a diverse array of actors, including government agencies, religious organizations, and private individuals, each with their own motivations and agendas. Settlement expansion has been facilitated by the construction of infrastructure, such as roads, schools, and housing units, as well as by the allocation of land and resources by Israeli authorities.

The growth of settlements has resulted in the displacement of Palestinian communities, the confiscation of land, and the fragmentation of the West Bank into disconnected enclaves, severely undermining the contiguity and viability of a future Palestinian state. Settlements are often built on confiscated Palestinian land, in violation of international law, and are connected by a network of bypass roads and security barriers that restrict Palestinian movement and access to resources.

The expansion of settlements in East Jerusalem, particularly in predominantly Palestinian neighborhoods, has further exacerbated tensions and contributed to the demographic and spatial transformation of the city. Israeli authorities have pursued policies of Judaization and demographic engineering, seeking to maintain Jewish demographic dominance in Jerusalem at the expense of Palestinian rights and aspirations.

Legal and Humanitarian Implications of the Occupation

The Israeli occupation of the West Bank and East Jerusalem has far-reaching legal and humanitarian implications under international law, including violations of fundamental human rights, breaches of international humanitarian law, and acts of colonization and annexation.

The Fourth Geneva Convention, adopted in 1949, prohibits the transfer of civilian populations into occupied territory and affirms the protection of civilians in times of conflict. The establishment of Israeli settlements in the West Bank and East Jerusalem constitutes a flagrant violation of this convention, as it involves the transfer of Israeli civilians into occupied territory and the appropriation of land for exclusively Israeli use.

The construction of settlements is also considered a violation of the principle of the prohibition of annexation of occupied territory, as enshrined in numerous United Nations resolutions and international legal instruments. Settlements alter the demographic composition of the occupied territories, undermine the rights and aspirations of the Palestinian population, and impede efforts to achieve a two-state solution based on the pre-1967 borders.

Moreover, the occupation has resulted in widespread human rights abuses and violations, including land confiscation, home demolitions, arbitrary detention, and restrictions on freedom of movement and expression. Palestinian communities living in the vicinity of settlements are subjected to constant harassment and intimidation by Israeli settlers and security forces, leading to a pervasive climate of fear and insecurity.

The humanitarian impact of the occupation is particularly acute in Gaza, where Israeli restrictions on the movement of people and goods have created a humanitarian crisis characterized by poverty, unemployment, and inadequate access to essential services such as healthcare and education. The blockade imposed by Israel on Gaza has resulted in severe shortages of food, medicine, and fuel, exacerbating the suffering of the civilian population and impeding reconstruction efforts following Israeli military operations.

International Responses and Resolutions

The growth of Israeli settlements and the ongoing occupation of the West Bank and East Jerusalem have been met with condemnation and calls for action from the international community, including the United Nations, the European Union, and individual states.

The United Nations Security Council has passed numerous resolutions condemning Israeli settlement activity and reaffirming the illegality of settlements under international law. Resolution 242, adopted in 1967, calls for the withdrawal of Israeli forces from territories occupied during the Six-Day War and the recognition of the sovereignty, territorial integrity, and political independence of all states in the region.

Resolution 2334, adopted in 2016, reiterates the illegality of Israeli settlements in the occupied Palestinian territories and calls for their immediate cessation. The resolution also calls on all states to distinguish, in their dealings with Israel, between the territory of the State of Israel and the territories occupied since 1967.

In addition to diplomatic efforts, civil society organizations, human rights groups, and grassroots activists have mobilized to raise awareness about the impact of settlements and the occupation on Palestinian rights and dignity. Boycott, Divestment, and Sanctions (BDS) campaigns have called for targeted economic and political pressure on Israel to end the occupation, dismantle settlements, and respect Palestinian rights.

However, despite international condemnation and efforts to hold Israel accountable for its actions, settlements continue to expand, and the occupation persists, with little prospect for meaningful change in the absence of a political resolution to the conflict. The failure of successive peace initiatives and the entrenchment of Israeli control over the occupied territories have deepened Palestinian disillusionment and despair, exacerbating tensions and perpetuating cycles of violence and insecurity.

In summary, the growth of Israeli settlements and the ongoing occupation of the West Bank and East Jerusalem represent major obstacles to peace and stability in the Israel-Palestine conflict. The expansion of settlements undermines the prospects for a viable two-state solution and perpetuates the dispossession and marginalization of the Palestinian people. Addressing the root causes of the conflict, including settlements and occupation, requires concerted international action, political will, and a commitment to upholding the principles of justice, equality, and human rights for all parties involved.

Chapter 8: Gaza Strip and Blockade

The Gaza Strip, a narrow coastal enclave bordered by Israel, Egypt, and the Mediterranean Sea, has been a focal point of the Israeli-Palestinian conflict for decades. This chapter delves into the significant events surrounding Gaza, including the Israeli disengagement in 2005, the rise of Hamas, and the resulting blockade, which has led to a humanitarian crisis in the region.

Israeli Disengagement from Gaza (2005)

In 2005, Israel undertook a unilateral disengagement plan from the Gaza Strip, which involved the evacuation of Israeli settlements and the withdrawal of Israeli military forces from the territory. The decision to disengage from Gaza was driven by a combination of security concerns, demographic considerations, and international pressure.

For nearly four decades, Israel maintained a presence in Gaza through military occupation and the establishment of Israeli settlements, which were built on land seized from Palestinians. The presence of Israeli settlers in Gaza exacerbated tensions and fueled violence, making the area a flashpoint for conflict between Israelis and Palestinians.

In August 2005, Israel implemented its disengagement plan, forcibly evacuating thousands of Israeli settlers from their homes in Gaza and dismantling settlements and military installations. The withdrawal was met with mixed reactions from both Israelis and Palestinians, with some viewing it as a step towards peace and others as a capitulation to terrorism.

The disengagement from Gaza was hailed by proponents as a bold and necessary move to improve Israel's security and pave the way for the eventual establishment of a Palestinian state. However, critics argued that the unilateral nature of the withdrawal, without coordination with the Palestinian Authority (PA) or agreement on final-status issues, risked exacerbating tensions and instability in the region.

Rise of Hamas in Gaza

Following the Israeli disengagement from Gaza, Palestinian political factions vied for control of the territory, leading to a power struggle between the secular nationalist Fatah movement, led by President Mahmoud Abbas, and the Islamist militant group Hamas.

Hamas, founded in 1987 as an offshoot of the Muslim Brotherhood, emerged as a potent political and military force in Gaza, capitalizing on widespread disillusionment with Fatah's perceived corruption and ineffectiveness. Hamas's extensive social welfare network, including schools, clinics, and charities, endeared it to many Palestinians, particularly in marginalized and impoverished communities.

In January 2006, Hamas scored a surprise victory in the Palestinian legislative elections, winning a majority of seats in the Palestinian Legislative Council (PLC) and ending Fatah's decades-long dominance of Palestinian politics. The election results reflected widespread discontent with Fatah's leadership and policies and signaled a desire for change among Palestinian voters.

Hamas's ascendance to power in Gaza posed a significant challenge to the Palestinian Authority and its efforts to negotiate a peace agreement with Israel. Unlike Fatah, which had pursued a strategy of negotiation and compromise, Hamas rejected the legitimacy of Israel and advocated for armed resistance against the occupation.

The Rise of Hamas in Gaza exacerbated tensions with Israel, leading to a series of confrontations and military escalations, including rocket attacks from Gaza and Israeli airstrikes and incursions. The cycle of violence and retaliation further deepened the divide between Israelis and Palestinians and hindered efforts to reach a negotiated settlement to the conflict.

Israeli Blockade and Humanitarian Crisis

In response to Hamas's rise to power in Gaza and continued rocket attacks against Israeli communities, Israel imposed a blockade on the territory in 2007, restricting the movement of goods and people in and out of Gaza and severely limiting access to essential services and resources.

The blockade, justified by Israeli authorities as a necessary security measure to prevent the smuggling of weapons and materials used for building rockets and tunnels, has had devastating humanitarian consequences for the civilian population of Gaza. The blockade has led to widespread poverty, unemployment, and food insecurity, with more than half of Gaza's population living below the poverty line.

Moreover, the blockade has severely restricted access to healthcare, education, and basic services, exacerbating already dire living conditions in the territory. Gaza's healthcare system, already overstretched and under-resourced, has struggled to cope with the influx of patients suffering from injuries and trauma as a result of Israeli military operations and the blockade-induced humanitarian crisis.

International humanitarian organizations and human rights groups have condemned the blockade as a collective punishment against the civilian population of Gaza and a violation of international law. The United Nations has called for an immediate end to the blockade and for unrestricted humanitarian access to Gaza to address the urgent needs of its residents.

Despite international condemnation and calls for action, the blockade remains in place, exacerbating the suffering of the people of Gaza and perpetuating cycles of violence and instability in the region. The humanitarian crisis in Gaza underscores the urgent need for a comprehensive and sustainable solution to the Israel-Palestine conflict that addresses the root causes of the conflict and respects the rights and dignity of all parties involved.

In summary, the Gaza Strip and the blockade imposed by Israel have been central to the Israeli-Palestinian conflict, with significant implications for the humanitarian situation and prospects for peace in the region. The Israeli disengagement from Gaza in 2005, the rise of Hamas, and the subsequent blockade have deepened divisions and tensions between Israelis and Palestinians, exacerbating an already volatile situation and hindering efforts to reach a just and lasting resolution to the conflict.

Chapter 9: Jerusalem: Contested City

Jerusalem stands as one of the most contested and revered cities in human history, with deep religious, historical, and political significance for Jews, Christians, and Muslims alike. This chapter delves into the multifaceted nature of Jerusalem, exploring its religious importance, the Israeli annexation of East Jerusalem, and the status of Jerusalem in peace negotiations between Israelis and Palestinians.

Religious Significance of Jerusalem

Jerusalem holds profound religious significance for three major monotheistic religions: Judaism, Christianity, and Islam. For Jews, Jerusalem is the holiest city in the world, revered as the site of the ancient Temple and the eternal capital of the Jewish people. The Western Wall, a remnant of the Second Temple, is one of Judaism's most sacred sites, serving as a place of pilgrimage, prayer, and reflection for Jews around the world.

For Christians, Jerusalem is associated with the life and teachings of Jesus Christ, making it a focal point of pilgrimage and devotion. The Church of the Holy Sepulchre, believed to be the site of Jesus' crucifixion, burial, and resurrection, is one of Christianity's holiest sites, attracting millions of pilgrims and visitors each year.

For Muslims, Jerusalem holds special significance as the third holiest city in Islam, after Mecca and Medina. The Dome of the Rock and the Al-Aqsa Mosque, located on the Temple Mount, are revered as sacred sites in Islam, associated with the Prophet Muhammad's Night Journey and Ascension to Heaven.

The religious significance of Jerusalem has fueled centuries of devotion, conflict, and reverence, making it a symbol of unity and division, hope and despair, for billions of believers around the world.

Israeli Annexation of East Jerusalem

Following the 1967 Six-Day War, Israel captured East Jerusalem, including the Old City and its holy sites, from Jordanian control and subsequently annexed it, in a move not recognized by the international community. The annexation of

East Jerusalem marked a significant departure from the status quo and sparked widespread condemnation and protests from the Arab world and the international community.

Israel's annexation of East Jerusalem was driven by a combination of religious, historical, and strategic motivations, including the desire to reunify the city, secure access to its holy sites, and establish Israeli sovereignty over the entire city. However, the annexation was met with fierce opposition from Palestinians, who view East Jerusalem as the capital of their future state and reject Israeli claims to the city.

The annexation of East Jerusalem has had profound legal, political, and humanitarian implications for the city and its residents. Palestinian residents of East Jerusalem are considered residents, not citizens, of Israel and face discrimination and marginalization in access to services, resources, and opportunities compared to their Jewish counterparts.

The annexation has also contributed to the fragmentation of Jerusalem, with Israeli settlements and infrastructure projects further dividing the city along ethnic and religious lines and undermining prospects for a negotiated resolution to the Israel-Palestine conflict.

Status of Jerusalem in Peace Negotiations

The status of Jerusalem has been one of the most contentious and sensitive issues in peace negotiations between Israelis and Palestinians, with both sides laying claim to the city as their capital. The Oslo Accords, signed in the 1990s, envisioned Jerusalem as a final-status issue to be negotiated between the parties, with the goal of achieving a two-state solution based on the pre-1967 borders.

However, efforts to reach a negotiated settlement on the status of Jerusalem have been stymied by deep-seated disagreements and competing narratives, with Israel insisting on its sovereignty over the entire city and Palestinians demanding East Jerusalem as the capital of their future state.

The United States' recognition of Jerusalem as the capital of Israel and its decision to relocate its embassy from Tel Aviv to Jerusalem in 2018 further inflamed tensions and undermined prospects for peace negotiations. The move was met with widespread condemnation from the international community, which viewed it as a violation of international law and a blow to efforts to achieve a negotiated settlement to the conflict.

Despite the challenges and obstacles to reaching a resolution on the status of Jerusalem, there remains a glimmer of hope for peace in the region. The city's rich history, religious significance, and cultural heritage serve as a powerful reminder of the common humanity and shared destiny of all who call Jerusalem home.

In conclusion, Jerusalem remains a contested city, caught in the crossfire of competing claims, aspirations, and visions for the future. The religious significance of Jerusalem, the Israeli annexation of East Jerusalem, and the status of Jerusalem in peace negotiations underscore the complexities and challenges of achieving a just and lasting resolution to the Israel-Palestine conflict. However, the enduring spirit of Jerusalem, as a city of peace, prayer, and pilgrimage, offers hope for a future where all who dwell in the city can live in harmony and mutual respect, honoring its sacred past and embracing its shared destiny.

Chapter 10: External Influences and Regional Dynamics

External influences and regional dynamics play a crucial role in shaping the Israel-Palestine conflict, influencing the policies, strategies, and actions of both Israeli and Palestinian actors. This chapter explores the role of neighboring Arab states, support from international actors such as the United States, the European Union, and the United Nations, and the impact of regional conflicts on the Israel-Palestine issue.

Role of Neighboring Arab States

Neighboring Arab states have historically played a significant role in the Israel-Palestine conflict, both as supporters of the Palestinian cause and as parties to regional conflicts with Israel. The attitudes and policies of key Arab states have evolved over time, reflecting changing geopolitical realities, strategic interests, and domestic considerations.

Egypt, one of the first Arab states to recognize Israel's existence following the signing of the Camp David Accords in 1979, has played a central role in mediating between Israelis and Palestinians and promoting peace in the region. The 1978 Camp David Accords and the subsequent 1979 Egypt-Israel Peace Treaty paved the way for Egypt to regain control of the Sinai Peninsula and establish diplomatic relations with Israel, albeit amid controversy and criticism from other Arab states.

Jordan, another neighboring Arab state, signed a peace treaty with Israel in 1994, becoming the second Arab country to formalize relations with Israel. The treaty, brokered by the United States, normalized diplomatic and economic ties between Jordan and Israel and led to increased cooperation in areas such as security, water management, and trade. However, public sentiment in Jordan remains largely sympathetic to the Palestinian cause, and the peace treaty with Israel remains a contentious issue in Jordanian politics.

Other Arab states, such as Saudi Arabia, the Gulf states, and Lebanon, have adopted varying positions on the Israel-Palestine conflict, reflecting a mix of pragmatism, ideology, and geopolitical considerations. While some Arab states have maintained a hardline stance against normalization with Israel until a comprehensive peace agreement is reached with the Palestinians, others have pursued closer ties with Israel as a means of countering shared threats such as Iran and extremism.

Overall, the role of neighboring Arab states in the Israel-Palestine conflict remains complex and multifaceted, with competing interests and priorities shaping their attitudes and actions towards the conflict and its resolution.

Support from International Actors: United States, European Union, United Nations

International actors, including the United States, the European Union, and the United Nations, have played a significant role in shaping the Israel-Palestine conflict, providing diplomatic, financial, and military support to both Israelis and Palestinians and seeking to advance peace and stability in the region.

The United States has long been a key player in the Israel-Palestine conflict, serving as a mediator, facilitator, and broker of peace negotiations between Israelis and Palestinians. The United States has provided extensive military aid and diplomatic support to Israel over the years, reflecting the close strategic alliance between the two countries and shared democratic values.

However, the United States' role as a mediator in the Israel-Palestine conflict has been criticized for its perceived bias towards Israel and its failure to hold Israel accountable for violations of international law and human rights abuses against Palestinians. The Trump administration's decision to recognize Jerusalem as the capital of Israel and relocate the U.S. embassy from Tel Aviv to Jerusalem in 2018 further inflamed tensions and undermined efforts to achieve a negotiated settlement to the conflict.

The European Union, a collective political and economic union of 27 European countries, has also been actively involved in efforts to promote peace and stability in the Middle East, including the Israel-Palestine conflict. The EU has provided significant financial assistance to the Palestinian Authority and supported initiatives aimed at promoting economic development, institution-building, and good governance in the Palestinian territories.

The European Union has consistently called for a two-state solution to the Israel-Palestine conflict, based on the pre-1967 borders, with Jerusalem as the capital of both Israel and a future Palestinian state. The EU has also condemned Israeli settlement expansion in the occupied territories and called for the lifting of the blockade on Gaza to alleviate the humanitarian crisis in the territory.

The United Nations, through its various agencies and bodies, has played a central role in addressing the Israel-Palestine conflict and advocating for the rights of Palestinians. The UN General Assembly and Security Council have adopted numerous resolutions condemning Israeli actions and calling for a peaceful resolution to the conflict based on international law and relevant UN resolutions.

The UN Relief and Works Agency for Palestine Refugees in the Near East (UNRWA) provides essential humanitarian assistance to Palestinian refugees and their descendants displaced by the 1948 Arab-Israeli war and subsequent conflicts. UNRWA operates schools, clinics, and social services in refugee camps across the Middle East, serving millions of Palestinians in need of assistance.

Despite international efforts to promote peace and stability in the region, progress towards a negotiated settlement to the Israel-Palestine conflict has been elusive, with deep-rooted divisions, distrust, and unresolved grievances persisting on both sides.

Impact of Regional Conflicts on the Israel-Palestine Issue

The Israel-Palestine conflict is deeply intertwined with broader regional conflicts and dynamics in the Middle East, including the Arab-Israeli conflict, the Israeli-Arab conflict, and the Israeli-Palestinian conflict. Regional conflicts and geopolitical rivalries have fueled tensions, violence, and instability in the region, exacerbating the complexities of the Israel-Palestine issue and hindering efforts to achieve a lasting resolution.

The Arab-Israeli conflict, which dates back to the early 20th century, has been a driving force behind the Israel-Palestine conflict, shaping the attitudes and policies of neighboring Arab states towards Israel and the Palestinians. The Arab-Israeli wars of 1948, 1967, and 1973, along with subsequent conflicts and confrontations, have left deep scars and lingering resentments, fueling mutual distrust and animosity between Israelis and Arabs.

The Israeli-Arab conflict, which encompasses the broader Arab-Israeli conflict as well as specific disputes between Israel and individual Arab states, has further complicated efforts to resolve the Israel-Palestine conflict. Peace treaties between Israel and Egypt and Jordan have brought partial normalization of relations between Israel and some Arab states but have failed to address the underlying issues of the Israeli-Palestinian conflict.

The ongoing conflict in Syria, the civil war in Yemen, and the regional rivalry between Iran and Saudi Arabia have also had significant implications for the Israel-Palestine issue, influencing alliances, strategies, and priorities of regional actors. The spread of extremism and terrorism, fueled by regional conflicts and sectarian tensions, has further destabilized the region and exacerbated the Israel-Palestine conflict.

The Israeli-Palestinian conflict has also been affected by the broader dynamics of the Middle East peace process, including efforts to resolve conflicts between Israel and its Arab neighbors and promote regional cooperation and integration. The normalization agreements between Israel and several Arab states in 2020, brokered by the United States under the Abraham Accords, marked a significant shift in regional dynamics and raised hopes for a new era of peace and cooperation in the Middle East.

However, the normalization agreements have been met with mixed reactions from Palestinians and the broader Arab world, with some viewing them as a betrayal of the Palestinian cause and a capitulation to Israeli interests. The absence of progress on the Israeli-Palestinian front and the continued expansion of Israeli settlements in the occupied territories have fueled frustration and disillusionment among Palestinians, undermining prospects for peace and stability in the region.

In conclusion, external influences and regional dynamics have played a pivotal role in shaping the Israel-Palestine conflict, influencing the attitudes, policies, and actions of key stakeholders in the region. The involvement of neighboring Arab states, support from international actors such as the United States, the European Union, and the United Nations, and the impact of regional conflicts have all contributed to the complexities and challenges of resolving the Israel-Palestine conflict. Moving forward, addressing the root causes of the conflict and fostering genuine dialogue, cooperation, and reconciliation among all parties involved will be essential for achieving a just and lasting peace in the Middle East.

Chapter 11: Humanitarian Consequences

The Israel-Palestine conflict has had profound humanitarian consequences for millions of people living in the region, including displacement and refugee crises, economic disparities and poverty, as well as psychological trauma and mental health impacts. This chapter examines these humanitarian consequences in detail, shedding light on the challenges faced by individuals and communities affected by the conflict.

Displacement and Refugee Crisis

The Israel-Palestine conflict has resulted in widespread displacement and a protracted refugee crisis, with millions of Palestinians forcibly displaced from their homes and denied the right to return under international law.

The Nakba, or "catastrophe," refers to the mass displacement of Palestinians during the 1948 Arab-Israeli war, when hundreds of thousands of Palestinians were expelled or fled from their homes as a result of the establishment of the State of Israel. Many Palestinians became refugees, seeking shelter and assistance in neighboring Arab countries or in refugee camps administered by the United Nations Relief and Works Agency for Palestine Refugees in the Near East (UNRWA).

The Nakba continues to reverberate through generations of Palestinians, with the descendants of refugees still living in refugee camps in the occupied territories, Jordan, Lebanon, and Syria. The right of return for Palestinian refugees, enshrined in United Nations General Assembly Resolution 194, remains a core issue in the Israel-Palestine conflict, with Palestinians demanding recognition of their right to return to their homes and properties from which they were displaced.

In addition to the Nakba, subsequent conflicts and Israeli military operations have resulted in further displacement and humanitarian crises in the occupied territories, particularly in the Gaza Strip and the West Bank. Israeli demolitions of Palestinian homes, land confiscations, and restrictions on movement and access to resources have exacerbated the plight of Palestinian communities, forcing many to seek refuge elsewhere or live in precarious conditions.

Economic Disparities and Poverty

The Israel-Palestine conflict has led to profound economic disparities and widespread poverty in the occupied territories, with Palestinians facing systemic discrimination, unemployment, and limited access to essential services and resources.

The Israeli occupation of the West Bank, including the construction of Israeli settlements and the establishment of military checkpoints and barriers, has disrupted Palestinian economic activity and hindered development, leading to stagnation and dependency on international aid. Palestinian businesses and farmers face numerous obstacles and restrictions imposed by Israeli authorities, including limits on movement, access to markets, and permits for construction and development.

In the Gaza Strip, the Israeli blockade and repeated military operations have devastated the local economy, causing widespread unemployment, poverty, and food insecurity. The blockade has restricted the movement of goods and people in and out of Gaza, severely limiting access to essential goods, services, and employment opportunities. The unemployment rate in Gaza is among the highest in the world, with over half of the population living below the poverty line.

The economic disparities between Israelis and Palestinians are stark, with Israelis enjoying significantly higher standards of living, access to education, healthcare, and employment opportunities compared to their Palestinian counterparts. The lack of economic opportunities and prospects for a better future has fueled frustration and despair among Palestinians, exacerbating tensions and instability in the region.

Psychological Trauma and Mental Health Impacts

The Israel-Palestine conflict has inflicted profound psychological trauma and mental health impacts on individuals and communities affected by violence, displacement, and oppression.

Palestinian children, in particular, have been exposed to high levels of trauma and violence, witnessing death, injury, and destruction at a young age. Studies have shown that a significant percentage of Palestinian children in the occupied territories suffer from symptoms of post-traumatic stress disorder (PTSD), anxiety, and depression, as a result of ongoing conflict and insecurity.

The psychological toll of the conflict extends beyond individuals to entire communities, with collective trauma and intergenerational transmission of trauma contributing to a cycle of violence and despair. Palestinian families and communities struggle to cope with the loss of loved ones, the destruction of homes and livelihoods, and the uncertainty of the future, leading to feelings of hopelessness and helplessness.

Israeli civilians living in communities near the Gaza Strip also face psychological challenges, including constant fear and anxiety about rocket attacks and violence from militant groups in Gaza. The trauma of living under the threat of violence and the loss of life and property have taken a toll on the mental health and well-being of residents, leading to increased rates of anxiety, depression, and PTSD.

The humanitarian consequences of the Israel-Palestine conflict underscore the urgent need for a comprehensive and sustainable solution that addresses the root causes of the conflict and promotes justice, equality, and human rights for all parties involved. Efforts to alleviate the suffering of affected communities, support economic development and recovery, and provide mental health support and trauma counseling are essential for building resilience and fostering hope for a better future in the region.

Chapter 12: Media and Propaganda

The role of media and propaganda in the Israel-Palestine conflict cannot be overstated. Media outlets, both traditional and digital, play a crucial role in shaping narratives, influencing public opinion, and framing the discourse surrounding the conflict. This chapter delves into the multifaceted dynamics of media and propaganda in the context of the Israel-Palestine conflict, exploring the role of media in shaping narratives, propaganda campaigns by both sides, and the challenges of objective reporting.

Role of Media in Shaping Narratives

Media outlets wield significant influence in shaping public perceptions and understanding of the Israel-Palestine conflict. Through news reports, opinion pieces, documentaries, and social media posts, media organizations frame events, highlight certain narratives, and amplify certain voices while marginalizing others.

Traditional media outlets such as newspapers, television networks, and radio stations play a central role in reporting on the conflict, providing analysis, commentary, and firsthand accounts of events on the ground. However, media coverage of the conflict often reflects the biases and editorial agendas of the outlets, leading to selective framing and polarization of narratives.

For example, Israeli media outlets tend to emphasize themes of national security, self-defense, and the threat of terrorism, portraying Israel as a beleaguered democracy fighting against existential threats from hostile neighbors and terrorist organizations. Palestinian media outlets, on the other hand, focus on themes of resistance, liberation, and national identity, highlighting the plight of Palestinians living under occupation and the struggle for self-determination.

Social media platforms have emerged as powerful tools for shaping public discourse and mobilizing support for different causes and perspectives. Platforms such as Twitter, Facebook, and Instagram enable individuals and organizations to share news, images, and videos in real-time, reaching millions of people around the world instantaneously.

However, social media platforms are also vulnerable to misinformation, propaganda, and manipulation, with both Israeli and Palestinian actors leveraging social media to disseminate their respective narratives and influence public opinion. The spread of fake news, doctored images, and inflammatory rhetoric on social media has further polarized the discourse surrounding the conflict, making it increasingly difficult to separate fact from fiction.

Propaganda Campaigns by Both Sides

Propaganda has been a key tool used by both Israeli and Palestinian actors to advance their respective agendas and shape public perceptions of the conflict. Propaganda campaigns often employ a range of tactics and techniques, including selective framing, emotional appeals, and the use of images and symbols to evoke sympathy and outrage.

Israeli propaganda efforts typically emphasize themes of security, self-defense, and the threat of terrorism, portraying Israel as a democracy under siege from hostile neighbors and terrorist organizations. Israeli propaganda campaigns seek to delegitimize Palestinian resistance and justify Israeli military actions and policies such as the blockade of Gaza and the construction of the West Bank barrier.

Palestinian propaganda efforts, on the other hand, focus on themes of resistance, liberation, and national identity, portraying Palestinians as victims of occupation and oppression struggling for their rights and freedom. Palestinian propaganda campaigns seek to highlight Israeli human rights abuses, violations of international law, and the plight of Palestinian refugees, garnering international sympathy and support for the Palestinian cause.

Both Israeli and Palestinian propaganda campaigns target domestic and international audiences through various channels, including traditional media, social media, public diplomacy, and grassroots activism. The goal of propaganda is to shape public perceptions, mobilize support for one's own cause, and undermine the legitimacy and credibility of the other side.

Challenges of Objective Reporting

Objective reporting on the Israel-Palestine conflict is fraught with challenges, including censorship, intimidation, and pressure from political actors and interest groups. Journalists operating in the region face numerous obstacles and risks, including physical violence, harassment, and legal threats, making it difficult to provide impartial and balanced coverage of the conflict.

Israeli authorities often impose restrictions on media access to the occupied territories, particularly in areas deemed sensitive or off-limits to journalists. Israeli military censorship and surveillance of media coverage inhibit journalists' ability to report freely and independently, leading to self-censorship and biased reporting.

Palestinian journalists also face challenges in reporting on the conflict, including censorship, harassment, and intimidation by Palestinian authorities and armed groups. Journalists critical of the Palestinian leadership or sympathetic to Israel risk arrest, detention, and even violence, making it difficult to report on sensitive issues and human rights abuses.

Moreover, the politicization of the Israel-Palestine conflict and the polarization of public opinion make it increasingly difficult for journalists to maintain objectivity and impartiality in their reporting. Journalists are often accused of bias and partisanship by supporters of one side or the other, leading to attacks on their credibility and professionalism.

Despite these challenges, many journalists and media organizations strive to uphold professional standards of journalism and provide accurate, balanced, and comprehensive coverage of the Israel-Palestine conflict. Independent media outlets, citizen journalists, and international news organizations play a crucial role in shedding light on the complexities of the conflict and amplifying the voices of those affected by violence, displacement, and oppression.

In conclusion, media and propaganda play a central role in shaping narratives and perceptions of the Israel-Palestine conflict, influencing public opinion, and shaping international responses to the issues at stake. However, the politicization of media coverage, the spread of misinformation, and the challenges of objective reporting pose significant obstacles to achieving a nuanced understanding of the conflict and its underlying causes. Efforts to promote media literacy, support independent journalism, and protect freedom of expression are essential for fostering informed dialogue and meaningful engagement on the Israel-Palestine issue.

Chapter 13: Grassroots Initiatives and Civil Society

Grassroots initiatives and civil society play a crucial role in fostering peace, reconciliation, and conflict resolution in the Israel-Palestine conflict. Amidst the backdrop of decades of political deadlock, violence, and diplomatic stalemate, grassroots movements and civil society organizations have emerged as beacons of hope, bringing together Israelis and Palestinians to promote dialogue, understanding, and cooperation. This chapter explores the diverse landscape of grassroots initiatives and civil society efforts in the Israel-Palestine conflict, highlighting peace movements, interfaith dialogue, reconciliation efforts, and the indispensable role of civil society in paving the way for a peaceful resolution to the conflict.

Peace Movements and Grassroots Organizations

Peace movements and grassroots organizations have long been at the forefront of efforts to promote peace, justice, and coexistence between Israelis and Palestinians. These movements, often led by activists, educators, and community leaders, seek to transcend political divides and bridge the gap between the two peoples through dialogue, education, and advocacy.

One prominent example of a grassroots peace movement is the Israeli-Palestinian Bereaved Families for Peace, also known as the Parents Circle-Families Forum. Founded in 1995 by Yitzhak Frankenthal, an Israeli whose son was killed by Palestinian militants, and Bassam Aramin, a Palestinian whose daughter was shot dead by Israeli border police, the Parents Circle-Families Forum brings together bereaved families from both sides of the conflict to promote reconciliation, understanding, and nonviolence. Through dialogue sessions, public events, and educational programs, the Parents Circle-Families Forum works to humanize the "other" and challenge stereotypes and prejudices, fostering empathy and solidarity among Israelis and Palestinians who have lost loved ones to the conflict.

Other grassroots organizations, such as Combatants for Peace, Women Wage Peace, and Seeds of Peace, also play a critical role in promoting peace and coexistence through grassroots activism, advocacy, and education. These organizations bring together Israelis and Palestinians from all walks of life to work towards a shared vision of peace, justice, and equality, challenging the status quo and advocating for concrete steps towards a negotiated settlement to the conflict.

Interfaith Dialogue and Reconciliation Efforts

Interfaith dialogue and reconciliation efforts serve as powerful catalysts for peace and understanding in the Israel-Palestine conflict, bringing together religious leaders, scholars, and practitioners from Jewish, Christian, and Muslim communities to promote dialogue, reconciliation, and mutual respect.

One notable example of interfaith dialogue and reconciliation efforts is the Interfaith Encounter Association (IEA), a grassroots organization founded in 2001 by Yehuda Stolov, an Israeli Jew, and Ghassan Manasra, a Palestinian Muslim, to promote interfaith dialogue, understanding, and cooperation among Israelis and Palestinians. The IEA organizes a wide range of programs and activities, including joint prayer sessions, study circles, and cultural exchanges, bringing together individuals from different religious backgrounds to engage in meaningful dialogue and build relationships based on trust and mutual respect.

Similarly, the Abrahamic Reunion, a grassroots network of Jewish, Christian, and Muslim spiritual leaders and activists, organizes interfaith events, peace pilgrimages, and solidarity visits to promote reconciliation, healing, and cooperation in the Holy Land. By transcending religious divides and emphasizing shared values and aspirations, the Abrahamic Reunion seeks to foster a culture of peace, compassion, and coexistence among Israelis and Palestinians.

Interfaith dialogue and reconciliation efforts also extend beyond formal organizations and initiatives, with religious leaders and institutions playing a crucial role in promoting peace and understanding within their respective communities. Rabbis, imams, and priests often serve as mediators, peacemakers, and advocates for dialogue and reconciliation, challenging stereotypes, promoting empathy, and fostering solidarity among their followers.

Role of Civil Society in Conflict Resolution

Civil society plays an indispensable role in conflict resolution and peacebuilding in the Israel-Palestine conflict, providing a platform for dialogue, collaboration, and advocacy at the grassroots level. Civil society organizations, including non-governmental organizations (NGOs), community groups, and grassroots movements, play a crucial role in mobilizing public support, raising awareness, and advocating for political change and social justice.

One example of the pivotal role of civil society in conflict resolution is the Geneva Initiative, a joint Israeli-Palestinian peace initiative launched in 2003 by prominent political figures, academics, and civil society leaders from both sides. The Geneva Initiative outlines a detailed framework for a negotiated settlement to the conflict, addressing key issues such as borders, security, refugees, and Jerusalem, based on the principles of international law, mutual recognition, and compromise. Through public outreach, education, and advocacy, the Geneva Initiative seeks to build grassroots support for a peace agreement and mobilize political leaders to take bold steps towards reconciliation and coexistence.

Civil society organizations also play a critical role in providing essential services and support to communities affected by the conflict, including humanitarian aid, psychosocial support, and legal assistance. Organizations such as Physicians for Human Rights-Israel, B'Tselem, and the Palestinian Center for Human Rights document human rights abuses, provide medical care to victims of violence, and advocate for justice and accountability on behalf of marginalized and vulnerable populations.

Moreover, civil society serves as a space for dialogue, debate, and dissent, allowing individuals and groups to express their grievances, aspirations, and demands, and hold political leaders and institutions accountable for their actions. Grassroots activism, advocacy campaigns, and social movements, such as the Boycott, Divestment, and Sanctions (BDS) movement and the Israeli-Palestinian Women's Peace Coalition, mobilize public support, raise awareness, and pressure governments and corporations to change their policies and practices in support of peace and justice.

In conclusion, grassroots initiatives and civil society play a vital role in promoting peace, reconciliation, and conflict resolution in the Israel-Palestine conflict. By bringing together Israelis and Palestinians from all walks of life, promoting interfaith dialogue, and advocating for political change and social justice, grassroots organizations and civil society movements contribute to building bridges of understanding, fostering empathy, and creating the conditions for a just and lasting peace in the region.

Chapter 14: Future Prospects and Challenges

The Israel-Palestine conflict has endured for decades, with numerous peace efforts and diplomatic initiatives failing to achieve a lasting resolution. As the conflict persists, the prospects for peace remain uncertain, while the challenges continue to evolve and intensify. This chapter explores the future prospects and challenges facing the Israel-Palestine conflict, including the debate between the two-state solution and the one-state solution, the challenges to peace posed by extremism, radicalization, and distrust, and potential pathways towards resolution.

Two-State Solution vs. One-State Solution

The debate between the two-state solution and the one-state solution lies at the heart of efforts to resolve the Israel-Palestine conflict. The two-state solution, which envisions the establishment of an independent Palestinian state alongside Israel, has long been the dominant framework for peace negotiations and diplomatic initiatives.

Proponents of the two-state solution argue that it offers the best chance for achieving a just and lasting peace, allowing Israelis and Palestinians to live side by side in security and dignity while addressing the legitimate national aspirations of both peoples. The two-state solution is based on the principles of territorial compromise, mutual recognition, and the creation of viable, contiguous, and sovereign states for Israelis and Palestinians.

However, the viability of the two-state solution has been increasingly called into question in recent years, as Israeli settlement expansion, territorial fragmentation, and political divisions have eroded the prospects for a viable Palestinian state. The continued construction of Israeli settlements in the occupied territories, particularly in East Jerusalem and the West Bank, has further entrenched Israeli control over Palestinian land and resources, making the establishment of a viable Palestinian state increasingly difficult.

In response to the challenges facing the two-state solution, some advocates and analysts have proposed alternative approaches, including the one-state solution. The one-state solution calls for the establishment of a single, democratic state in historic Palestine, where Israelis and Palestinians would enjoy equal rights and citizenship.

Proponents of the one-state solution argue that it offers a more just and equitable solution to the conflict, addressing the root causes of inequality, discrimination, and dispossession that have fueled decades of violence and oppression. By transcending ethnic and religious divides and embracing principles of democracy and equality, the one-state solution seeks to create a shared future for Israelis and Palestinians based on principles of justice, reconciliation, and coexistence.

However, critics of the one-state solution raise concerns about its feasibility and viability, citing the deep-seated mistrust, historical grievances, and demographic challenges that would need to be overcome to realize such a vision. The one-state solution also raises questions about the preservation of national identity, cultural autonomy, and security for Israelis and Palestinians, as well as the practical challenges of governance, administration, and representation in a unified state.

Challenges to Peace: Extremism, Radicalization, and Distrust

The prospects for peace in the Israel-Palestine conflict are further complicated by the presence of extremism, radicalization, and distrust on both sides of the divide. Extremist groups and individuals, motivated by nationalist, religious, or ideological agendas, seek to perpetuate violence, undermine peace efforts, and sabotage any prospects for reconciliation and coexistence.

On the Israeli side, extremist settlers, militant groups, and far-right political parties advocate for the annexation of the occupied territories, the expulsion of Palestinians, and the imposition of exclusive Jewish control over historic Palestine. These groups reject the notion of Palestinian statehood and advocate for the continued expansion of Israeli settlements as a means of asserting Jewish sovereignty over the land.

Similarly, on the Palestinian side, extremist factions, militant organizations, and Islamist movements such as Hamas reject the legitimacy of Israel, advocate for armed resistance, and seek to establish an Islamic state in place of Israel.

These groups reject the Oslo Accords and other peace initiatives, viewing them as capitulation to Israeli occupation and betrayal of the Palestinian cause.

Extremism and radicalization are fueled by a sense of injustice, marginalization, and dispossession experienced by both Israelis and Palestinians, as well as by the absence of political progress and the perpetuation of violence and insecurity. Extremist rhetoric and actions further exacerbate tensions, deepen divisions, and undermine trust between the two sides, making it increasingly difficult to build consensus and forge a path towards peace.

Distrust and suspicion between Israelis and Palestinians also pose significant obstacles to peace, perpetuating cycles of violence, retaliation, and escalation. Years of conflict, violence, and mutual suffering have engendered deep-seated mistrust and animosity between the two peoples, making it difficult to overcome historical grievances and forge meaningful partnerships for peace.

Moreover, the lack of mutual recognition, understanding, and empathy between Israelis and Palestinians perpetuates stereotypes, prejudices, and misperceptions, reinforcing negative attitudes and perceptions towards the "other" and hindering efforts to build bridges of understanding and cooperation.

Potential Pathways towards Resolution

Despite the daunting challenges and obstacles facing the Israel-Palestine conflict, there remain potential pathways towards resolution that offer hope for a peaceful and just resolution to the conflict. These pathways require bold leadership, political will, and international support, as well as a commitment to dialogue, negotiation, and compromise from all parties involved.

First and foremost, a renewed commitment to the two-state solution is essential for achieving a just and lasting peace in the region. Efforts to revive the two-state solution must address the root causes of its decline, including Israeli settlement expansion, Palestinian fragmentation, and political deadlock, while reaffirming the principles of mutual recognition, territorial compromise, and the creation of viable, contiguous, and sovereign states for Israelis and Palestinians.

To revive the two-state solution, Israeli and Palestinian leaders must engage in meaningful negotiations based on the relevant UN resolutions, the principles of international law, and previous agreements and understandings reached between the two sides. Negotiations must address key issues such as borders, security, Jerusalem, refugees, and settlements, while addressing the legitimate concerns and aspirations of both Israelis and Palestinians.

In addition to diplomatic efforts, grassroots initiatives and civil society organizations play a crucial role in building trust, fostering dialogue, and promoting reconciliation between Israelis and Palestinians. By bringing together individuals and communities from both sides, grassroots movements create opportunities for face-to-face encounters, shared experiences, and meaningful interactions that challenge stereotypes, humanize the "other," and foster empathy and understanding.

Interfaith dialogue and reconciliation efforts also serve as important pathways towards resolution, bringing together religious leaders, scholars, and practitioners from Jewish, Christian, and Muslim communities to promote dialogue, understanding, and cooperation. By emphasizing shared values and principles, interfaith initiatives create spaces for mutual respect, tolerance, and solidarity, transcending religious divides and fostering a culture of peace and coexistence in the Holy Land.

International support and engagement are essential for advancing peace and reconciliation in the Israel-Palestine conflict. The international community, including the United Nations, the European Union, the United States, and regional actors, must reaffirm their commitment to a negotiated settlement based on the principles of international law, UN resolutions, and the two-state solution.

Moreover, international actors have a responsibility to hold parties accountable for violations of human rights and international law, including settlement construction, land confiscation, and the use of excessive force against civilians. By upholding international norms and standards, the international community can create incentives for compliance, deterrence for violations, and leverage for diplomatic progress towards peace.

In conclusion, the future prospects for peace in the Israel-Palestine conflict depend on the collective efforts of Israelis, Palestinians, and the international community to overcome the challenges and obstacles that stand in the way of a just and lasting resolution. While the road ahead is fraught with difficulties, there are several key steps that can be taken to advance the cause of peace and reconciliation in the region.

Firstly, it is essential for all parties involved to demonstrate a genuine commitment to dialogue, negotiation, and compromise. This requires courageous leadership on both the Israeli and Palestinian sides, willing to make difficult concessions in pursuit of peace. Negotiations must be conducted in good faith, with a recognition of the legitimate rights and aspirations of both peoples.

Secondly, efforts to address the root causes of the conflict, including Israeli settlement expansion, Palestinian displacement, and security concerns, must be prioritized. This may involve freezing settlement construction, dismantling illegal outposts, and implementing confidence-building measures to rebuild trust between the two sides.

Thirdly, steps must be taken to address the humanitarian and socio-economic needs of the Palestinian population, particularly those living in Gaza and the West Bank. This includes lifting the blockade on Gaza, easing restrictions on movement and access, and investing in infrastructure, healthcare, and education to improve living conditions and promote economic development.

Fourthly, efforts to combat extremism, radicalization, and incitement must be intensified. This requires a comprehensive approach that addresses the underlying grievances and grievances driving extremism, while promoting tolerance, moderation, and respect for human rights and the rule of law.

Fifthly, regional and international actors must play a constructive role in facilitating peace negotiations and supporting efforts to build trust and confidence between Israelis and Palestinians. This may involve diplomatic initiatives, economic incentives, and security guarantees to create an enabling environment for peace.

Finally, it is crucial to recognize the role of civil society, grassroots movements, and interfaith initiatives in promoting peace and reconciliation at the local level. These actors play a vital role in building bridges of understanding, fostering dialogue, and promoting mutual respect and coexistence between Israelis and Palestinians.

In conclusion, while the challenges facing the Israel-Palestine conflict are formidable, there are reasons for hope and optimism. With courage, commitment, and collective action, it is possible to overcome the obstacles to peace and build a future based on justice, equality, and mutual respect for all peoples in the region. The road ahead may be long and arduous, but the goal of a just and lasting peace is worth pursuing with determination and resolve.

Chapter 15: Conclusion

The Israel-Palestine conflict stands as one of the most enduring and complex conflicts of our time, spanning generations and defying resolution despite numerous peace efforts and diplomatic initiatives. As we reflect on the multifaceted dynamics of this conflict, it becomes clear that its roots run deep, entrenched in a complex web of historical, political, religious, and territorial factors. In this concluding chapter, we will reflect on the enduring nature of the conflict, the importance of ongoing dialogue and international engagement, and the hope for a peaceful resolution and lasting reconciliation.

Reflection on the Enduring Nature of the Conflict

The Israel-Palestine conflict is characterized by its deep-seated historical roots, marked by competing narratives, territorial disputes, and conflicting national aspirations. From ancient times to the present day, the land of historic Palestine has been a battleground for competing claims and identities, with each side invoking historical, religious, and cultural narratives to justify their presence and rights to the land.

The conflict is further complicated by the legacy of colonialism, imperialism, and the displacement of indigenous peoples, as well as by the failure of previous peace initiatives and the perpetuation of violence, oppression, and human rights abuses on both sides. Decades of occupation, dispossession, and conflict have left deep scars on the land and its people, fueling cycles of violence, mistrust, and despair that have proven difficult to overcome.

Moreover, the Israel-Palestine conflict is intertwined with broader regional and international dynamics, including geopolitical rivalries, security concerns, and the interests and agendas of external actors. The involvement of neighboring Arab states, regional powers, and international actors has further complicated efforts to achieve a peaceful resolution to the conflict, adding layers of complexity and uncertainty to an already volatile situation.

Despite numerous attempts to address the root causes of the conflict, including peace negotiations, diplomatic initiatives, and international interventions, the Israel-Palestine conflict persists, defying easy solutions and perpetuating human suffering and insecurity for millions of people in the region.

Importance of Ongoing Dialogue and International Engagement

In the face of such entrenched conflict and complexity, the importance of ongoing dialogue and international engagement cannot be overstated. Dialogue serves as a crucial tool for building understanding, empathy, and trust between Israelis and Palestinians, fostering a culture of peace, coexistence, and mutual respect.

Dialogue initiatives, such as Track II diplomacy, people-to-people exchanges, and grassroots peacebuilding efforts, create opportunities for individuals and communities from both sides to engage in meaningful dialogue, share perspectives, and build relationships based on common humanity and shared aspirations for peace. By humanizing the "other" and challenging stereotypes and prejudices, dialogue initiatives help bridge divides and lay the groundwork for reconciliation and coexistence.

International engagement is equally essential for addressing the Israel-Palestine conflict, given its implications for regional stability, global security, and the promotion of human rights and international law. The international community, including the United Nations, the European Union, the United States, and regional actors, has a responsibility to support efforts to achieve a just and lasting resolution to the conflict, based on the principles of international law, UN resolutions, and the two-state solution.

International actors can play a constructive role in facilitating peace negotiations, providing political and economic incentives for compliance, and holding parties accountable for violations of human rights and international law. Moreover, international engagement is essential for addressing the humanitarian and socio-economic needs of the Palestinian population, including humanitarian assistance, development aid, and support for institution-building and capacity-building efforts.

Hope for a Peaceful Resolution and Lasting Reconciliation

Despite the challenges and complexities of the Israel-Palestine conflict, there remains hope for a peaceful resolution and lasting reconciliation between Israelis and Palestinians. The desire for peace and security is shared by ordinary people on both sides, who yearn for an end to violence, oppression, and insecurity, and for a future based on justice, equality, and mutual respect.

The pursuit of peace requires courage, commitment, and leadership from all parties involved, as well as a willingness to make difficult concessions and compromises in pursuit of a common goal. It also requires a recognition of the legitimate rights and aspirations of both Israelis and Palestinians, including the right to self-determination, security, and dignity.

A just and lasting resolution to the Israel-Palestine conflict must address the root causes of the conflict, including Israeli occupation, Palestinian dispossession, and the denial of basic rights and freedoms for Palestinians living under occupation. It must also address the legitimate security concerns of Israel, including the threat of terrorism and violence against its citizens.

Moreover, a just and lasting resolution to the conflict must be based on the principles of international law, including the relevant UN resolutions, the Geneva Conventions, and the Universal Declaration of Human Rights. It must also be guided by the principles of mutual recognition, territorial compromise, and the creation of viable, contiguous, and sovereign states for Israelis and Palestinians.

In conclusion, while the Israel-Palestine conflict remains one of the most intractable conflicts of our time, there is reason to hope for a peaceful resolution and lasting reconciliation between Israelis and Palestinians. Through ongoing dialogue, international engagement, and a commitment to justice and human rights, it is possible to overcome the barriers to peace and build a future based on coexistence, mutual respect, and shared prosperity for all peoples in the region. Despite the entrenched nature of the conflict, there have been moments of progress and signs of hope that demonstrate the possibility of a peaceful resolution.

One such moment was the signing of the Oslo Accords in 1993, which marked a historic breakthrough in Israeli-Palestinian relations and raised hopes for a negotiated settlement to the conflict. While the Oslo process ultimately faltered and failed to achieve its objectives, it demonstrated the potential for dialogue and negotiation to bring about positive change and build trust between the two sides.

Similarly, the Arab Peace Initiative, first proposed by Saudi Arabia in 2002 and subsequently endorsed by the Arab League, offers a comprehensive framework for a regional peace settlement, including the normalization of relations between Israel and the Arab states in exchange for a full Israeli withdrawal from the occupied territories and a just solution to the Palestinian refugee issue. While the Arab Peace Initiative has yet to be fully realized, it remains a viable pathway towards regional peace and stability.

In recent years, there have also been grassroots initiatives and civil society efforts that have sought to promote peace and reconciliation at the local level. Organizations such as Parents Circle-Families Forum, Combatants for Peace, and Women Wage Peace have brought together Israelis and Palestinians from all walks of life to engage in dialogue, build trust, and work towards a shared vision of peace. While these initiatives face significant challenges and obstacles, they demonstrate the resilience and determination of ordinary people to overcome divisions and build bridges of understanding and cooperation.

Looking ahead, the path to peace in the Israel-Palestine conflict will require sustained commitment, creativity, and perseverance from all parties involved. It will require bold leadership, willing to make difficult decisions and compromises in the pursuit of peace. It will require the support and engagement of the international community, including regional actors, global powers, and civil society organizations, to facilitate negotiations, provide incentives for peace, and hold parties accountable for their actions.

Ultimately, the quest for peace in the Israel-Palestine conflict is a moral imperative, rooted in the principles of justice, equality, and human dignity. It is a vision of a future where Israelis and Palestinians can live side by side in peace and security, sharing the land they both call home in mutual respect and harmony. While the road ahead may be long and challenging, the goal of a just and lasting peace is worth pursuing with unwavering determination and resolve.

In conclusion, as we reflect on the enduring nature of the Israel-Palestine conflict, we are reminded of the urgent need for continued dialogue, international engagement, and a commitment to justice and human rights.

Despite the obstacles and challenges that lie ahead, there is reason to hope for a peaceful resolution and lasting reconciliation between Israelis and Palestinians. Through perseverance, empathy, and a shared commitment to peace, it is possible to overcome the divisions and build a future based on coexistence, mutual respect, and shared prosperity for all peoples in the region.

Don't miss out!

Visit the website below and you can sign up to receive emails whenever Michael Johnson publishes a new book. There's no charge and no obligation.

https://books2read.com/r/B-A-OREFB-FXWZC

BOOKS 2 READ

Connecting independent readers to independent writers.